D1104071

Where
the
Sidewalk
Ends

the poems and drawings of
Shel Silverstein

CHILDREN'S
STORYTELLERS

Shel
Silverstein

by Chris Bowman

Note to Librarians, Teachers, and Parents:

Blastoff! Readers are carefully developed by literacy experts and combine standards-based content with developmentally appropriate text.

Level 1 provides the most support through repetition of high-frequency words, light text, predictable sentence patterns, and strong visual support.

Level 2 offers early readers a bit more challenge through varied simple sentences, increased text load, and less repetition of high-frequency words.

Level 3 advances early-fluent readers toward fluency through increased text and concept load, less reliance on visuals, longer sentences, and more literary language.

Level 4 builds reading stamina by providing more text per page, increased use of punctuation, greater variation in sentence patterns, and increasingly challenging vocabulary.

Level 5 encourages children to move from "learning to read" to "reading to learn" by providing even more text, varied writing styles, and less familiar topics.

Whichever book is right for your reader, Blastoff! Readers are the perfect books to build confidence and encourage a love of reading that will last a lifetime!

This edition first published in 2016 by Bellwether Media, Inc.

No part of this publication may be reproduced in whole or in part without written permission of the publisher. For information regarding permission, write to Bellwether Media, Inc., Attention: Permissions Department, 5357 Penn Avenue South, Minneapolis, MN 55419.

Library of Congress Cataloging-in-Publication Data

Bowman, Chris, 1990-
    Shel Silverstein / by Chris Bowman.
        pages cm. – (Blastoff! Readers: Children's Storytellers)
    Summary: " Simple text and full-color photographs introduce readers to Shel Silverstein. Developed by literacy experts for students in kindergarten through third grade "– Provided by publisher.
    Includes bibliographical references and index.
    Audience: Ages 5-8
    Audience: K to grade 3
    ISBN 978-1-62617-271-5 (hardcover: alk. paper)
    1. Silverstein, Shel–Juvenile literature. 2. Authors, American–20th century–Biography–Juvenile literature. 3. Illustrators–United States–Biography–Juvenile literature. 4. Children's literature–Authorship–Juvenile literature. I. Title.
    PS3569.I47224Z57 2016
    818'.54–dc23
    [B]
                                            2015005172

Printed in the United States of America, North Mankato, MN.

Table of Contents

Who Was Shel Silverstein?

Shel Silverstein was the creative mind behind many children's stories and poems. He also wrote songs, plays, and books for adults.

Shel's stories connect with kids through humor. They joke about things like adults and their rules. Because of this, his books continue to be popular with children today.

fun fact

Shel wrote more than 800 songs!

"I was always prepared for success but that means that I have to be prepared for failure too."

Shel Silverstein

A Wandering Mind

Shel Silverstein was born on September 25, 1930. He grew up in Chicago, Illinois, with his parents and younger sister.

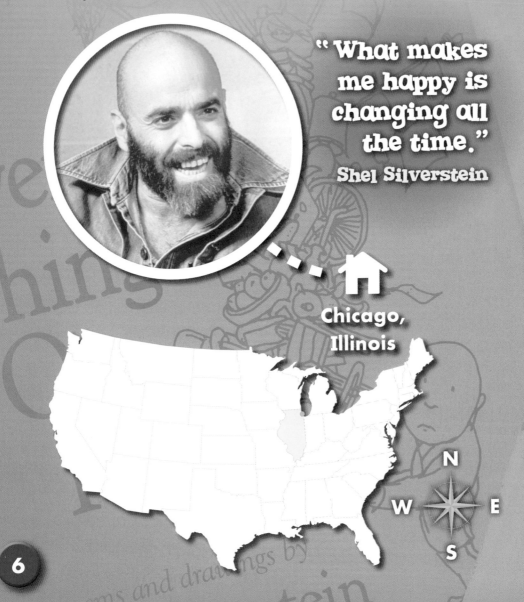

"What makes me happy is changing all the time."
Shel Silverstein

Chicago, Illinois

Shel often liked to be alone. He
listened to the radio and read books
and **comic strips**. He learned to draw
by tracing the comics in the newspaper.

"I just walked around a lot and made up stories in my head. Then I'd go home and write them down. That's how I got started."
Shel Silverstein

At home, Shel's father wanted him to help out with the family business. But Shel only wanted to read and draw. They argued often.

In the classroom, Shel had a hard time paying attention to lessons. Instead, he liked to draw and make up stories.

fun fact
Shel's favorite comic strip was *Li'l Abner* by Al Capp.

After high school, Shel went to college. But he had trouble finding a school he liked. By 1953, he had tried three different schools. He left college when he was **drafted** into the United States Army.

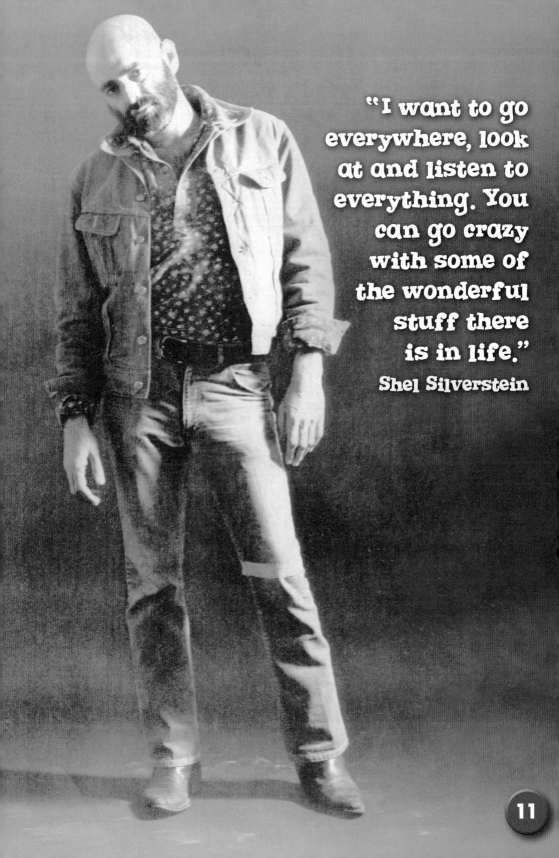

"I want to go everywhere, look at and listen to everything. You can go crazy with some of the wonderful stuff there is in life."

Shel Silverstein

In the Army, Shel was **stationed** in Japan and South Korea. But he still found time to draw. He worked for the Army's newspaper. It printed many of his cartoons.

Japan

South Korea

N

W E

S

Shel's cartoons covered the daily lives of soldiers **abroad**. They quickly became popular with readers. In 1955, the Army **published** a book of Shel's cartoons. Later that year, he was **discharged** from the Army.

A Creative Genius

Back in Chicago, Shel tried to sell his cartoons to magazines. His father still disagreed with his **career** choice. But Shel knew he could be successful. After many months, magazines finally began buying his work.

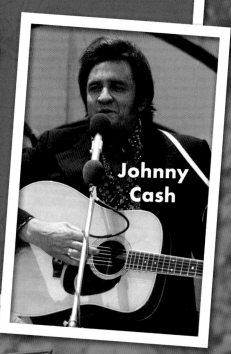
Then Shel moved to New York. He continued writing and drawing. He also found success in new areas. He tried singing, songwriting, and painting. Soon, a friend suggested he write books for children.

In 1963, Shel published his first children's book, called *Lafcadio: The Lion Who Shot Back*. The next year, he published three more stories for kids. They were hits! He went on to write several more children's best sellers.

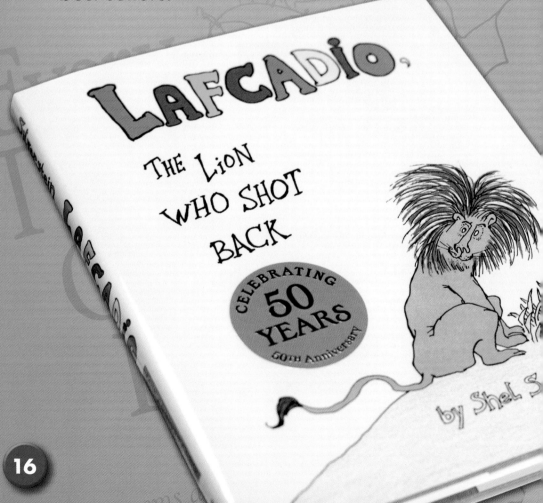

SELECTED WORKS

Lafcadio: The Lion Who Shot Back (1963)

The Giving Tree (1964)

Who Wants a Cheap Rhinoceros? (1964)

A Giraffe and a Half (1964)

Where the Sidewalk Ends (1974)

The Missing Piece (1976)

The Missing Piece Meets the Big O (1981)

A Light in the Attic (1981)

Falling Up (1996)

Runny Babbit (2005)

Shel wanted kids to use their imaginations. He created wacky characters for his stories. His books also encouraged kids to be different.

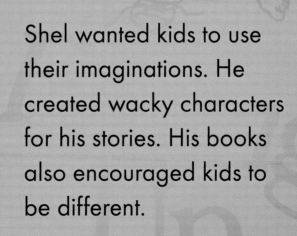

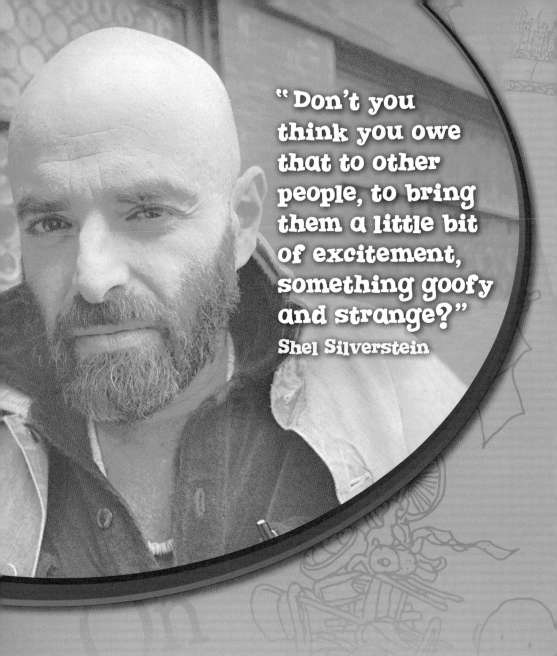

"Don't you think you owe that to other people, to bring them a little bit of excitement, something goofy and strange?"
Shel Silverstein

Shel thought that kids were too often told what to do. He wanted his readers to be able to think for themselves. Because of this, he left endings open in his stories.

Shel also thought children's books had too many happy endings. He wanted to be honest with his readers. Life can be both happy and sad. Many of his stories are both.

The Tree Keeps Giving

It has been more than 50 years since Shel's first children's book came out. Kids still love reading his writing.

"Do something you love, time will pass, and you'll have fun."
Shel Silverstein

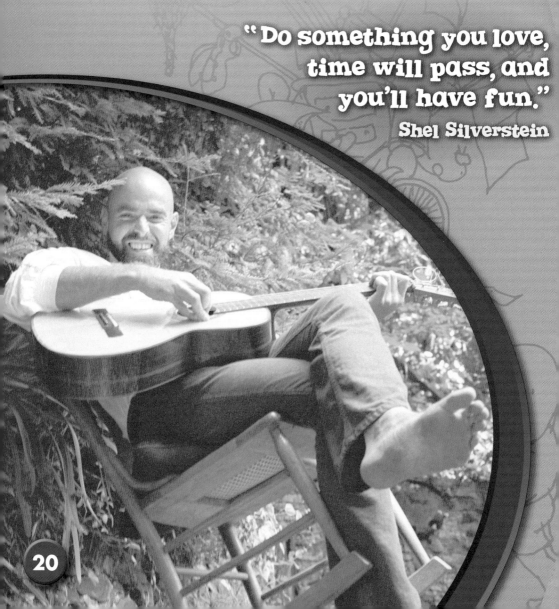

IMPORTANT DATES

1930: Shel is born on September 25, in Chicago, Illinois.

1955: The Army's newspaper publishes a book of Shel's cartoons called *Take Ten*.

1956: Shel sells his first cartoons to a magazine.

1963: *Lafcadio: The Lion Who Shot Back*, Shel's first children's book, is published.

1974: *Where the Sidewalk Ends* wins the *New York Times* Outstanding Book for Children Award.

1981: *A Light in the Attic* begins its 182-week run as a *New York Times* best seller.

1984: Shel wins the Best Children's Album Grammy Award for *Where the Sidewalk Ends*.

1991: One of Shel's songs, "I'm Checking Out," is nominated for an Academy Award.

1999: Shel passes away on May 10th in Key West, Florida.

2005: *Runny Babbit*, a book Shel had worked on for many years, is published and wins the Quill Award for Children's Illustrated Books.

His silly poems and stories still relate to childhood experiences today. Shel's creativity will continue to **inspire** young readers for years to come.

Glossary

abroad—in a foreign country

career—a job someone does for a long time

comic strips—brief series of drawings in panels that are funny or that tell a story

discharged—let go from duty

drafted—called to military service

inspire—to give someone an idea about what to do or create

published—printed work for a public audience

stationed—sent to a certain place for a period of time

To Learn More

AT THE LIBRARY

Haney, Johannah. *Shel Silverstein*. New York, N.Y.: Cavendish Square Publishing, 2014.

Kolpin, Molly. *Shel Silverstein*. Mankato, Minn.: Capstone Press, 2014.

Silverstein, Shel. *Where the Sidewalk Ends: The Poems & Drawings of Shel Silverstein*. New York, N.Y.: HarperCollins, 2004.

ON THE WEB
Learning more about Shel Silverstein is as easy as 1, 2, 3.

1. Go to www.factsurfer.com.

2. Enter "Shel Silverstein" into the search box.

3. Click the "Surf" button and you will see a list of related web sites.

With factsurfer.com, finding more information is just a click away.

Index

The images in this book are reproduced through the courtesy of: Everett Collection/ Newscom/ Alamy, front cover, pp. 6, 9; Bellwether Media, front cover (book covers, background), all interior backgrounds, p. 16; Alice Ochs/ Getty Images, pp. 4-5, 8, 14-15, 20; rook76, p. 7; Sarah Marchant, p. 10; Gems/ Getty Images, p. 11; Jeff Albertson/ Corbis, pp. 13, 18; JP Laffont/ Sygma/ Corbis, p. 15; Tampa Bay Times/ ZUMA Press, p. 19.

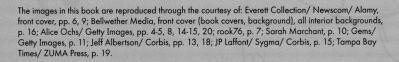